TO THE POINT. AGILE

TO THE POINT.

'**TO THE POINT.**' books cut through the clutter, simplifying complexity for an easy understanding of core concepts—no fluff, just clarity.

CONTENTS

WHAT IS AGILE

Agile is a set of values and principles in software development prioritizing collaboration, flexibility, and customer satisfaction.

It advocates an iterative and incremental approach, enabling teams to efficiently respond to changing requirements and deliver valuable software.

THREE REASONS TO BE AGILE

1 INCREASED FLEXIBILITY & ADAPTABILITY

2 ENHANCED COLLABORATION & COMMUNICATION

3 IMPROVED QUALITY & CUSTOMER SATISFACTION

AGILE MANIFESTO

The Agile Manifesto guides teams toward customer-centric and effective delivery through its values and principles, serving as the cornerstone of Agile.

1 INDIVIDUALS & INTERACTIONS
over processes and tools

2 WORKING SOFTWARE
over comprehensive documentation

3 CUSTOMER COLLABORATION
over contract negotiation

4 RESPONDING TO CHANGE
over following a plan

AGILE MANIFESTO PRINCIPLES

Simplified Agile Manifesto principles:

- **Satisfy customers** by delivering early and continuously.
- **Embrace changing requirements** for a competitive advantage.
- **Deliver working software frequently** with shorter timescales.
- **Collaborate** with customers and stakeholders.
- Build projects around **motivated individuals**, providing trust and support.
- Prioritize **face-to-face** communication.
- Measure progress by **working software.**
- **Promote sustainable development** for sponsors, developers, and users.
- Continuous attention to **technical excellence**.
- Let **simplicity** maximize the amount of work not done.
- The best outcomes come from **self-organizing teams.**
- **Regularly reflect and adjust** for increased effectiveness.

SCRUM DEFINED

Scrum is an Agile framework designed for product development, particularly in software, is versatile across industries. It offers a structured, flexible approach to project and product management, emphasizing iterative progress, collaboration, and adaptability.

Key components of Scrum:

- **Roles:** Distinguished to ensure accountability and efficient collaboration.
- **Events (Ceremonies):** Vital for team collaboration, progress assessment, and strategy refinement, promoting communication and transparency.
- **Artifacts:** Essential for prioritizing work and representing incremental progress.
- **Timeboxed Iterations (Sprints):** Typically lasting 1-4 weeks.
- **Empirical Process Control:** Important for continuous improvement, using real-time feedback through transparency, inspection, and adaptation in processes.

SPRINT DEFINED

Scrum is centred around the concept of **'Sprints', fixed-duration iterations** during which a team works to deliver an increment of a product that can potentially be shipped.

Scrum emphasizes iterative and incremental development which allow teams to deliver valuable increments, collect feedback, and adapt to changing requirements.

Key aspects of a Sprint:

- **Short Iterations:** Typically 1 to 4 weeks, determined by the team based on project nature and historical performance.
- **Clear Goals and Priorities:** At the start of the sprint, the team selects items from the Product Backlog to form the Sprint Backlog.
- **Potentially Shippable Increment:** The primary sprint goal is delivering a potentially shippable product increment.
- **Inspect and Adapt:** At the end of the sprint, a Review showcases completed work, and a Retrospective identifies areas for improvement.
- **No Changes During the Sprint:** Once a sprint starts, chosen work and goals remain fixed, ensuring focus and commitment..

KANBAN DEFINED

Kanban, originating in Japan at Toyota, has evolved into a versatile approach adopted in various industries, including software development. It aims to **visualize work**, limit work-in-progress, and enhance overall efficiency and flow.

Core principles of Kanban:

- **Visualize Work:** Display tasks for easy tracking and workflow understanding.
- **Limit Work-in-Progress (WIP):** Set explicit task limits to prevent overload and maintain a smooth workflow.
- **Manage Flow:** Optimize workflow, identify bottlenecks, and eliminate them for efficient delivery.
- **Foster a Culture of Continuous Improvement:** Regularly review and adapt for ongoing efficiency enhancements.

ITERATIVE VS INCREMENTAL

Iterative and incremental development are two distinct approaches in software development, each emphasizing specific aspects of the development process.

- **Iterative Development:** Focuses on refining the entire product through continuous feedback loops, emphasizing continuous improvement of the product.
- **Incremental Development:** Focuses on gradually adding new features by breaking down the product into functional pieces and delivering them incrementally, emphasizing gradual feature additions.

Both approaches are often combined, creating a development cycle that is both iterative and incremental, fostering flexibility and steady growth.

SCRUM 3-4-5

Scrum emphasizes adaptability and continuous improvement through iterative and collaborative development with defined roles, events, and artifacts.

3 ROLES

- Product Owner
- Scrum Master
- Development Team

4 EVENTS

- Sprint Planning
- Sprint Review
- Sprint Retro
- Daily Stand-up

5 ARTIFACTS

- Product Backlog
- Sprint Backlog
- Definitions Of
- Product Increment
- Burndown Chart

3 ROLES

- Product Owner
- Scrum Master
- Development Team

4 EVENTS

- Sprint Planning
- Sprint Review
- Sprint Retro
- Daily Stand-up

5 ARTIFACTS

- Product Backlog
- Sprint Backlog
- Definitions Of
- Product Increment
- Burndown Chart

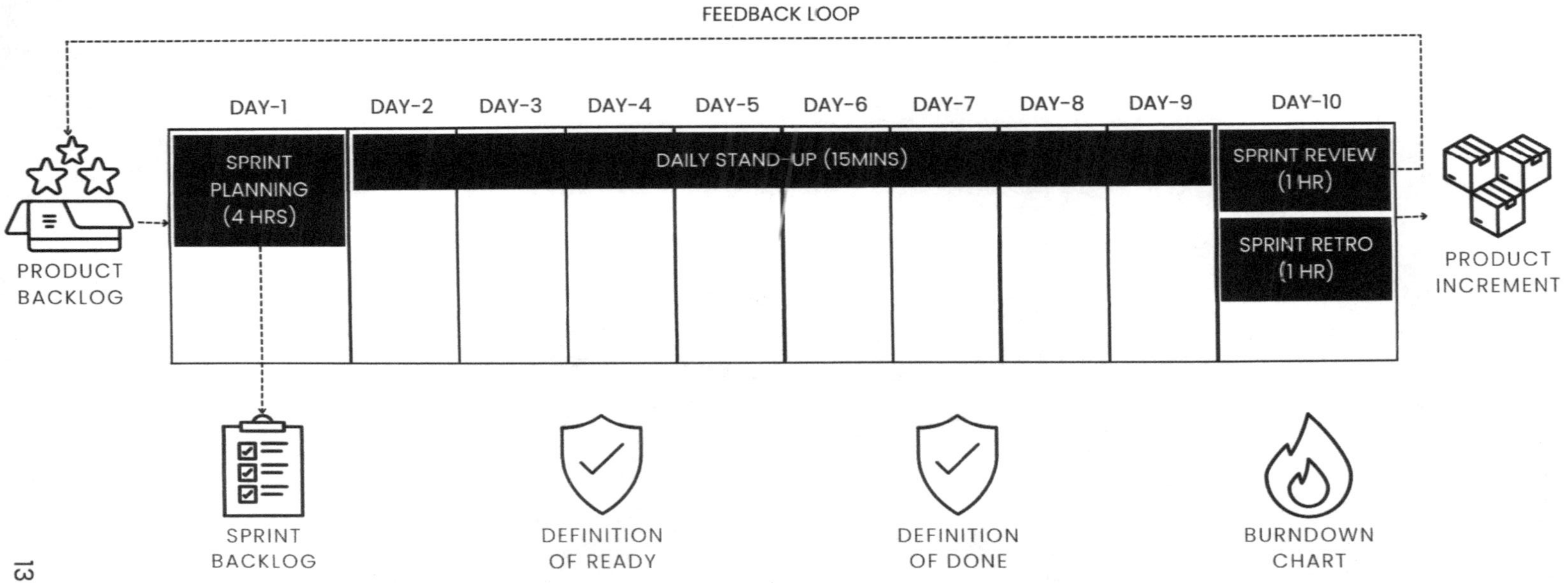

PRODUCT INCREMENT

FEEDBACK LOOP

DAY-1	DAY-2	DAY-3	DAY-4	DAY-5	DAY-6	DAY-7	DAY-8	DAY-9	DAY-10

SPRINT PLANNING (4 HRS)

DAILY STAND-UP (15MINS)

SPRINT REVIEW (1 HR)

SPRINT RETRO (1 HR)

PRODUCT BACKLOG

SPRINT BACKLOG

DEFINITION OF READY

DEFINITION OF DONE

BURNDOWN CHART

3 ROLES

Maintaining a team size of 5-9 members is optimal to ensure effective communication, collaboration, and to avoid challenges associated with small and large teams.

PRODUCT OWNER

Serves as the representative of the customer, sets product priorities, and aligns development with customer needs.

SCRUM MASTER

Facilitates Scrum, ensures adherence, overcomes obstacles, and fosters streamlined development.

DEVELOPMENT TEAM

Delivers high-quality product increments and drives product success through a cross-functional unit.

PRODUCT OWNER

The Product Owner plays a critical role tasked with **prioritizing customer needs**, defining a clear and compelling product vision, and collaborating with the team to create a dynamic backlog for incremental value delivery.

Key aspects of the Product Owner role:

- **Customer-focused:** Advocate for customer requirements.
- **Visionary:** Align the product vision with organizational goals.
- **Ownership:** Collaborate on a clear product backlog.
- **Transparency:** Communicate priorities and respond promptly to team queries.
- **Partnership:** Encourage open communication and build strong partnerships with the Scrum Master and Development Team.
- **Adaptive:** Adjust priorities based on feedback and market shifts.
- **Value-focused:** Prioritize features for maximum value and aim for incremental delivery in each sprint.
- **Improvement:** Identify areas for improvement and foster a culture of continuous learning.

SCRUM MASTER

The Scrum Master plays an important role in **guiding and facilitating** effective collaboration, continuous improvement, and adherence to Agile principles within the team.

Key aspects of the Scrum Master role:

- **Facilitation:** Ensure effective team collaboration during Scrum events.
- **Resolution:** Lead resolution of obstacles hindering team progress.
- **Empowerment:** Empower the Development Team for self-organization.
- **Servant-Leadership:** Lead by serving team needs and creating support.
- **Champion:** Champion a culture of continuous improvement.
- **Protection:** Safeguard the team from external disturbances.
- **Adherence:** Ensure consistent adherence to Scrum principles.
- **Encouragement:** Promote open communication and collaboration within the team.

DEV TEAM

The Development Team is vital in turning Product Backlog items into valuable products. As a cross-functional, self-organizing unit, they are fully committed to **delivering high-quality products** in each sprint.

Key aspects of the Development Team role:
- **Cross-functional:** Leverage diverse skills for optimal results.
- **Commitment:** Fully commit to achieving sprint goals.
- **Accountability:** Take ownership of tasks and contribute proactively to team success.
- **Improvement:** Seek opportunities to enhance processes and deliver greater value.
- **Adherence:** Rigorously adhere to quality standards defined by the team.
- **Openness:** Foster an open environment for sharing ideas and insights through transparent communication.
- **Participation:** Actively participate in decision-making processes leveraging collective insights.
- **Learning:** Use feedback as a tool for learning and refining contributions to the team's success.

4 EVENTS

Agile events are important touchpoints in iterative development, fostering collaboration, transparency, and continuous improvement for successful delivery outcomes.

 SPRINT PLANNING

 SPRINT REVIEW

 SPRINT RETROSPECTIVE

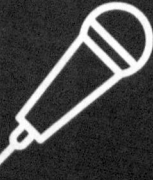 DAILY STAND-UP

SPRINT PLANNING

Sprint Planning establishes a **clear direction for the upcoming sprint** through collaborative decision-making, aligning the team on sprint goals and priorities.

Part 1: Sprint Goal and Priority Setting

The Product Owner presents sprint goal and highest priority Product Backlog items.

Part 2: Sprint Backlog Confirmation

Development Team estimates effort, confirms items based on capacity (velocity), and breaks them into tasks to form the Sprint Backlog.

Duration: 1 to 4 hours (recommended 2 hours per week of the sprint duration).

Frequency: Once per sprint (at the start).

Attendees: Product Owner, Scrum Master, Development Team, and Subject Matter Experts (when required).

SPRINT PLANNING

Roles and Responsibilities during Sprint Planning:

Product Owner - Customer Representative

Leads the discussion about the Product Backlog, clarifies priorities, and defines the sprint goal.

Scrum Master - Facilitator

Facilitates the meeting, ensures collaboration, and maintains focus on the sprint goal.

Development Team - Participants

Actively participate in the backlog discussion, contribute to goal-setting, and collaborate on task breakdown and estimation.

Subject Matter Experts (when required)

Offer domain-specific insights crucial for task breakdown and capacity planning.

AGILE ESTIMATION
PART OF SPRINT PLANNING

Agile estimation in Sprint Planning assesses the effort and complexity of user stories for informed sprint scope decisions.

Key principles of Agile Estimation:

- **Relativity:** Evaluate complexity using relative estimation values like story points or t-shirt sizing.
- **Collectiveness:** Foster collaboration among all Development Team members for diverse perspectives and collective agreement on estimates.
- **Iterative:** Regularly conduct iterative refinement to adjust estimates based on evolving information, maintaining accuracy throughout implementation
- **Consistency:** Uphold sizing consistency for reliable planning aligned with the team's work capacity (velocity).

Agile Estimation Techniques:

- **Planning Poker:** Improves accuracy through diverse perspectives, allowing independent estimates and converging collectively for a team estimate.
- **Fibonacci Sequence:** Facilitates relative estimations with Fibonacci numbers (1, 2, 3, 5, 8, 13, etc.), emphasizing differences in complexity.
- **Reference Stories:** Ensures consistency and benchmarking for a shared understanding in new user stories.

PLANNING POKER
PART OF SPRINT PLANNING

Planning Poker is an Agile estimation technique commonly used during Sprint Planning to collectively estimate the effort or complexity of user stories.

Steps for Planning Poker:

1. **Preparation:** Familiarize the team with the user story and use Planning Poker cards
2. **Round Initialization:** The facilitator presents a user story for discussion.
3. **Individual Estimation:** Each team member privately selects an estimate.
4. **Simultaneous Reveal:** Everyone reveals their cards simultaneously.
5. **Discussion and Clarification:** Discuss divergent estimates and align the team's understanding.
6. **Re-Estimation (Optional):** Repeat steps 3 to 5 if needed to reach a consensus.
7. **Consensus and Final Estimate:** Aim for consensus and agree on a final estimate.
8. **Record Estimate:** Capture the agreed estimate for the user story.
9. **Repeat:** Repeat steps 2 to 8 for all selected user stories.

CAPACITY PLANNING

PART OF SPRINT PLANNING

Capacity Planning in Agile relies on **'Velocity,' a metric quantifying the team's productivity**. It indicates completed work in story points per sprint, guiding Sprint Planning based on average velocity.

Key aspects of Velocity:

- **Consistency:** Rely on consistent estimation and relative complexity against reference stories.
- **Completeness:** Focus on completed work for a realistic view of team's productivity.
- **Variability:** Allow velocity variation between sprints due to factors like team composition and work complexity.

Calculation:

- Velocity is calculated by summing up the story points of completed user stories within a single sprint.
- Average Velocity = $\dfrac{\text{Total Story Points of Completed Sprints}}{\text{Number of Completed Sprints}}$

SPRINT REVIEW

Sprint Review **inspect and adapts the Product Increment** with stakeholders to encourage collaboration and gather feedback for improving future iterations.

Part 1: Demonstration
A demonstration of the Product Increment, ensuring alignment with stakeholder expectations.

Part 2: Feedback and Adaptation
Collaborative session with stakeholders and team members to discuss improvements, adjustments, and lessons learned.

Duration: 1 to 2 hours (recommended 0.5 hours per week of the sprint duration).
Frequency: Once per sprint (at the end).
Attendees: Product Owner, Scrum Master, Development Team, Stakeholders, and Subject Matter Experts (when relevant).

SPRINT REVIEW

Roles and Responsibilities during Sprint Review:

Product Owner - Customer Representative

Leads the demonstration, gathers feedback, and collaborates on refining the product backlog based on insights.

Scrum Master - Facilitator

Facilitates the session and stakeholder feedback, and encourages collaboration for continuous improvement.

Development Team - Demonstrators

Performs the demonstration, responds to stakeholder queries, and engages in feedback discussions for iterative refinement.

Stakeholders - Reviewers

Provide feedback, share expectations, and contribute insights to align the product with organizational goals and user needs.

SPRINT RETRO

Sprint Retrospective aims to **reflect on the team's performance** and identify improvement opportunities.

Part 1: Reflection and Insights
Open discussion on successes and challenges, encouraging positive reflections.

Part 2: Improvement Planning
Collaboratively identify actionable improvements and establish a plan for implementation in the next sprint.

Duration: 1 to 2 hours (recommended 0.5 hours per week of the sprint duration).
Frequency: Once per sprint (at the end).
Attendees: Product Owner, Scrum Master, and Development Team.

SPRINT RETRO

Roles and Responsibilities during Sprint Retrospective:

Product Owner - Participant

Participates in discussions, provides insights on the impact of Sprint outcomes on product goals, and collaborates on improvement planning.

Scrum Master - Facilitator

Guides the team through the retrospective process, encourages active participation and helps in identifying improvement opportunities.

Development Team - Participants

Actively engages in reflections, shares perspectives on challenges faced, and contributes to identifying and implementing improvements.

DAILY STAND-UP

The Daily Stand-up ensures **daily team alignment**, quick progress updates, and prompt resolution of potential roadblocks or issues.

The Daily Stand-up involves team members answering **three key questions:**

1. What did I **accomplish yesterday?**
2. What will I **work on today?**
3. Are there any obstacles or **impediments** in my way?

Duration: 15 mins.

Frequency: Daily (start of the day).

Attendees: Development Team, Scrum Master, and Product Owner (optional).

DAILY STAND-UP

Roles and Responsibilities during Daily Stand-up:

Product Owner (Optional) - Silent Observer

Attends to stay informed, providing input or clarification when needed.

Scrum Master - Facilitator

Removes impediments raised during the stand-up, ensures focus on the three questions and fosters collaboration.

Development Team - Participants

Share progress updates, discuss roadblocks, and collaborate on issue resolution.

5 ARTIFACTS

Artifacts play integral roles in planning, tracking progress, and delivering value, ensuring a transparent and effective development process.

PRODUCT BACKLOG

SPRINT BACKLOG

DEFINITIONS OF

PRODUCT INCREMENT

BURNDOWN CHART

PRODUCT BACKLOG

The Product Backlog is a **comprehensive list of work items** defining the product, guiding the development team in aligning the product with customer needs and business goals.

Key characteristics of a Product Backlog:

- **Comprehensive List:** Includes epics, user stories, defects, and enhancements.
- **Prioritized:** Items ranked based on significance to product and business goals.
- **Refined:** Maintained and regularly refined by the Product Owner.
- **Dynamic:** Continuously updated to reflect changing priorities, market conditions, and feedback.
- **Collaborative:** Developed with input from the Product Owner, stakeholders, and the Development Team.

EPICS

PART OF PRODUCT BACKLOG

Epics are **strategic components of the Product Backlog**, representing large, high-level user stories or themes with a broad scope. Typically too large for a single sprint, they are broken down into smaller user stories.

Key characteristics of epics:

- **Strategic:** Provide a strategic view of major features shaping the product roadmap.
- **Complex:** Involve substantial size and complexity, unsuitable for a single sprint.
- **High-Level:** Positioned above user stories, serving as high-level themes broken down for sprint implementation.
- **Adaptable:** Subject to refinement based on changing priorities, impacting detailed user stories.
- **Collaborative:** Defined collaboratively by the Product Owner, stakeholders, and the Development Team for shared understanding and alignment.

USER STORIES
PART OF PRODUCT BACKLOG

User stories, forming part of the Product Backlog, **capture user needs and benefits** by focusing on individual functionality. They contribute to product incrementally and guide the team in implementation

Key characteristics of user stories:
- **Independent:** Describes a single functionality.
- **Negotiable:** Allows flexibility in implementation.
- **Valuable:** Contributes to overall product value.
- **Estimable:** Can be estimated for development effort.
- **Small:** Represents a manageable unit of work.
- **Testable:** Clearly defined acceptance criteria for completion.

Rules of thumb for writing effective user stories:
- **INVEST**: Ensure user stories are Independent, Negotiable, Valuable, Estimable, Small, and Testable.
- **User-centric**: Focus on user needs, avoiding technical details.
- **Clarity:** Use the "As a [Role], I want [Action], So that [Benefit]" template for clarity.
- **3C:** Create the Card, engage in Conversations, and define acceptance criteria (Confirmation).
- **Vertical-slicing:** Focus on end-to-end functionality and value.

SPRINT BACKLOG

The Sprint Backlog is a **subset of the Product Backlog**, consisting of user stories chosen by the Development Team for a specific sprint. It serves as a comprehensive plan for the work to be completed during the sprint.

Key characteristics of a Sprint Backlog:

- **Prioritized:** User stories are selected based on priority, feasibility, and capacity during Sprint Planning.
- **Deliverable:** User stories are discussed, estimated, and agreed upon to be deliverable within a sprint.
- **Detailed:** User stories are often broken down into tasks for guidance during sprint execution.

DEFINITION OF READY

The Definition of Ready is a **set of criteria** that a user story must meet **before it is accepted into a sprint**. It ensures that the team has all the necessary information and conditions in place to start working on a user story effectively.

A typical "Definition of Ready" of an user story includes:

- **Description:** Provides a concise narrative outlining the specific needs, actions, and benefits.
- **Acceptance Criteria:** Clearly outlines the conditions that must be met for the user story to be considered complete.
- **Prioritization:** Prioritized based on business value and goals.
- **Approval:** The user story has been reviewed and accepted as ready for implementation by the Product Owner.

DEFINITION OF DONE

The Definition of Done is a **set of criteria** that a user story must meet to be **considered complete and ready for release**. It ensures that the team and stakeholders share a common understanding of the quality and completeness of the work.

A typical "Definition of Done" of a user story includes:

- **Code Quality:** Implementing working code that undergoes peer review to meet quality standards.
- **Unit Tests:** Ensuring that unit tests validate the functionality of the implemented code.
- **Integration Tests:** Confirming seamless integration with the overall system by passing integration tests.
- **Regression Tests:** Verifying that existing functionality remains unaffected.
- **Acceptance Criteria:** Meeting all acceptance criteria outlined in the user story.
- **Documentation:** Updating relevant documentation to reflect changes.
- **Approval:** Showcasing the working product for Product Owner's approval and alignment with stakeholder expectations.

www.ingramcontent.com/pod-product-compliance
Lightning Source LLC
Chambersburg PA
CBHW050525290526
45786CB00007B/2699

CLEAR MIND

CLEAR MIND is on a mission to unravel complexity with simplicity, offering digestible insights and practical guidance to empower individuals in realizing their full potential.

PRODUCT INCREMENT

A Product Increment is a functional output which represents a version of the **product that is potentially shippable**, showcasing the cumulative work completed by the Development Team in previous sprints.

Key characteristics of a Product Increment:

- **Valuable:** Enhance overall functionality with measurable value in each increment bringing tangible benefits to users or stakeholders.
- **Shippable:** Attain a state where the increment is ready for potential release to customers.
- **Cumulative:** Builds on top of the features delivered in previous increments.
- **Complete:** Consider the increment complete by meeting the Definition of Done.

BURNDOWN CHART

A Burndown Chart visually represents the **amount of work completed versus work remaining** during a sprint. It gives a overview of the team's progress in achieving their sprint goal.

Key components of a Burndown Chart:

- **Progress Tracking:** Visualise completed work versus remaining work provide to track the team's schedule status.
- **Productivity Trends:** Identifies trends in team productivity for early intervention or adjustments as needed.
- **Forecasting Capability:** Enables the team to forecast the completion of planned work by the end of the sprint.

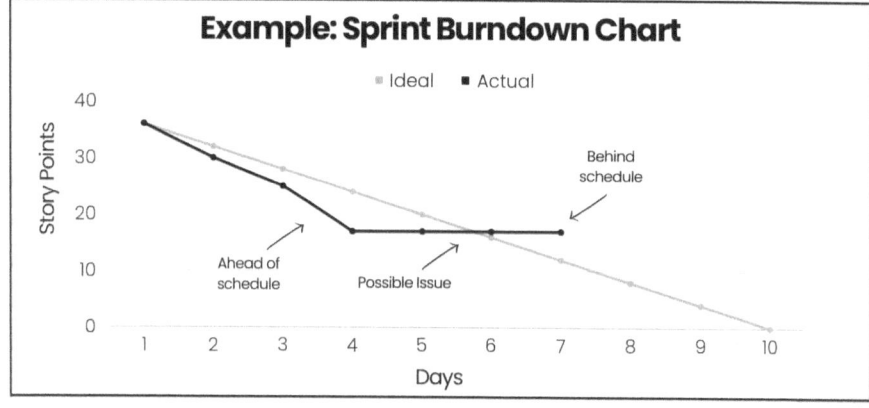

- **Time Axis:** Duration of the sprint.
- **Work Axis:** Remaining work (story points or hours).
- **Ideal Burndown Line:** Ideal rate of completion.
- **Actual Burndown Line:** Actual rate of completion.